Online Marketing Success!

Your Pyramid to Website Success!

Jim Rudnick MCSD

Rudnick Press

ISBN: 978-0-9939410-0-9

Rudnick Press

For my Susan with love and more...

OUR GO-TO-MARKET ONLINE MARKETING STRATEGY

[A Strategy for Start-Ups]

Our basic belief in being a practicing online marketing executive is the simple one that for anything to work, one must first "plan" your work and then on a regular basis, "work your plan!"

To do that, we have learned over the past 35 years that the planning of an online marketing campaign takes skill is based on empirical evidence. Evidence that over those years, we gathered from staying as close to the leading edge of "what works" for online marketing by being in touch with other experts, analyzing client campaigns and tactics to upgrade our strategic thinking and then reading and researching bulletin boards, message boards, forums and now

blogs...it's a constant part of our day and that information is never accepted on behalf of our clients without full testing and analysis – it's that process we've found to work.

What follows herein, is a set of foundational building blocks for anyone looking to develop their own website's online marketing plan based on our tried and true testing of scheduled tasks.

What we will be doing over the next sessions, is trying to impart to you, what you need to consider, to ponder and to think/rethink in creating your own targeted go-to-market online strategy for your own online business.

Jim Rudnick
2014

Table of Sessions & Contents

❖ **Opening Session & Executive Summary/Rationale**

Website Foundations

1.0 Monthly Website Foundation Tasks

1.1 – Website Aesthetics

1.2 – Products & Services

1.3 – Call to Actions

1.4 – Conversion Tracking

❖ **Search Engine Optimization Strategy/Tactics**

2.0 Weekly SEO Foundation Tasks

2.1 – Keyword Research

2.2 – On Page Optimization

2.3 – Off Page Optimization

❖ **Social Media Strategy/Tactics**

3.0 Daily Social Media Foundation Tasks

3.1 – Social Media Authority

3.2 – Social Media Community

❖ **Online Monitoring/Tweaking/Resets**

4.0 Monitoring & Analytics Task

❖ **5.0 Online Go-To-Market Program Summation**

Executive Summary

What we will be doing over this book, is to try to impart to you, what you need to consider, to ponder and to think/rethink in creating your own targeted go-to-market online strategy for your own online business.

What does your Audience want from You?

First, you need to realize that you are trying to provide a unique service or a product to your marketing universe...

And you know exactly what your audiences may be searching for to find your wares....

- But do you know what they really want out of you?
- Do you know how they really feel?
- Do you know what they want more of or less of in your industry?
- Do you know what they like or don't like on your site or your competitor's sites?
- Do you know what they think about your new product launch?

If you knew this information, how could you use it to improve your products or services?

[http://en.wikipedia.org/wiki/Push%E2%80%93pull_strategy]

What do You want from your Audience?

You provide something to them, but what is it you want back in return?

Is it money? Is this venture how you intend to make your living and pay your bills?

Is it fame? Are you looking to be the next famous founder who sells out but becomes famous when doing so? Like Bronfman or Bell from previous generations, or Haney or Abbot from Trivial Pursuit or Ted Livingston of Kik Messenger or the list is endless.

Is it a more 'social' rationale perhaps, a green or community based desire to succeed?

Is that what you're after? Money? Fame? Respect? And the authority that comes with it? Responsibility too!

You need to decide on that too for a host of reasons because that has – and I will show – a direct bearing on how you "engage" your audience…your customers…your clients.

1.0 Monthly Website Foundation Tasks

As the basic building block of a successful online marketing program begins with your website, it is most important to build a website that considers the following factors...

Marketing Strategy Foundation Factors ~

- 90% of people search online before making decisions to buy products or services

- To do that, they visit your website and look at what you are offering

- You need to have an aesthetically pleasing site that offers up both your products and services as well as some sort of customer/client reviews or testimonials

- You will need therefore to have a call-to-action that will allow the prospective customer/client to make the decision to buy from your website

- And you will also need to monitor your website via analytics to ensure that the site is working up to its full potential

1.1 – Website Aesthetics

Usability

Website usability involves building a site which is easy, fun, and logical for users, so that they can enjoy using the site and they can utilize it to find what they need. This consideration is critically important for companies that want to build brand loyalty and attract customers, as people are turned off by websites which they have trouble using. Make it simple for a potential new client or customer to make an inquiry or to buy your products/services.

Photos, colors, contrast, graphics and layout are aesthetic elements that enhance communication of information. The visual form of these elements on your website depends on the ideas you want to communicate to your potential customers. Ideas you might articulate include "**_trust this company_**," "**_buy this product_**," "**_read this information_**," "**_explore this area_**," or "**_take this trial_**" etc. We integrate your objectives with aesthetic elements to achieve a desirable website atmosphere that will effectively communicate ideas and information to your customers.

Best practices for aesthetic website design

- Create visual clues based on groupings; related items or links are grouped together while unrelated items are separated.

- Use headings and subheadings to allow visual scanning of content.

•Use headings, subheadings, font sizes, bold fonts and italic fonts in proportion to the importance of the item.

•Align elements on a page so that they are all visually connected; size all elements on the page to create balance and unity; nothing should look out of place unless you have a specific reason for the effect.

•Choose a font style that supports the site atmosphere and stick to it; limit styles to 2 at the most.

•Use images and photos for visual appeal and to communicate ideas.

•Use one set of design elements across your website.

OMG – Aesthetically Unpleasing:

- [http://www.zyra.org.uk/]
- [http://www.bearflagwine.com/]
- [http://www.pandminc.com/] flash!

YES – Aesthetically Pleasing:

- [http://www.blueacorn.com/]
- [http://fatbellyburgers.com/]
- [http://www.emotionslive.co.uk/]

Usability Testing –[
http://en.wikipedia.org/wiki/Usability_testing]

Goals of usability testing:

Usability testing is a black-box testing technique. The aim is to observe people using the product to discover errors and areas of improvement. Usability testing generally involves measuring how well test subjects respond in four areas: efficiency, accuracy, recall, and emotional response. The results of the first test can be treated as a baseline or control measurement; all subsequent tests can then be compared to the baseline to indicate improvement.

- *Performance* -- How much time, and how many steps, are required for people to complete basic tasks? (For example, find something to buy, create a new account, and order the item.)

- *Accuracy* -- How many mistakes did people make? (And were they fatal or recoverable with the right information?)

- *Recall* -- How much does the person remember afterwards or after periods of non-use?

- *Emotional response* -- How does the person feel about the tasks completed? Is the person confident, stressed? Would the user recommend this system to a friend?

Usability testing methods:

1]. Hallway testing --

Hallway testing (or **Hall Intercept Testing**) is a general methodology of usability testing. Rather than using an in-house, trained group of testers, just five to six random people, indicative of a cross-section of end users, are brought in to test the product, or service. The name of the technique refers to the fact that the testers should be random people who pass by in the hallway.

2]. Remote testing --

Remote testing, which facilitates evaluations being done in the context of the user's other tasks and technology can be either synchronous or asynchronous. Synchronous usability testing methodologies involve video conferencing or employ remote application sharing tools such as **WebEx**. The former involves real time one-on-one communication between the evaluator and the user, while the latter involves the evaluator and user working separately. Numerous tools are available to address the needs of both these approaches. **WebEx and Go-to-meeting** are the most commonly used technologies to conduct a synchronous remote usability test.

3]. Expert review --

Expert review is another general method of usability testing. As the name suggests, this method relies on bringing in experts with experience in the field (possibly from companies that specialize in usability

testing) to evaluate the usability of a product, **which can be an expensive process to gather this data for startups!**

Resources & Testing URLS -

[http://usability.jameshom.com/index.htm]

[http://www.smashingmagazine.com/2009/05/15/optimizing-conversion-rates-its-all-about-usability/]

[http://en.wikipedia.org/wiki/Website_architecture]

[http://en.wikipedia.org/wiki/Web_design]

[http://en.wikipedia.org/wiki/Interaction_design]

[http://www.usabilityfirst.com/about-usability/]

Navigation

Navigation remains one of the most critical aspects of Web site design – and in my book, arguably the most important. No matter how good a site looks, and no matter how much useful information it offers, if it doesn't have a sensible navigation scheme, it will confuse visitors and chase them away.

Remember – users either think "easy" – or – they "vote with their feet!"

A simple, logical, understandable navigation scheme can increase your number of page impressions, boost return visits, and improve your **"conversion rate"** (the number of visitors who are "converted" into customers). It's a critical aspect of site design that has a direct effect on the bottom line.

Information architecture is the work that goes into creating intuitive navigation schemes for software. Information architecture generally applies to websites, but can also apply to web applications, mobile applications, and social media software.

Ideally, a website or application's navigation scheme makes it easy for users to find desired information or functionality. On a website, the information architecture can also add important context to the current page (for example when a user begins their visit deep within the website, having come directly from a search engine).

A "bricks and mortar" architect must balance the (often competing) demands of aesthetics, structural integrity, heating, lighting, water supply and drainage when creating building blueprints. Similarly, an information architect must create navigation schemes for software that are at once concise, descriptive, mutually-exclusive, and possessive of information scent. Both types of architect seek to create spaces for humans that are safe, predictable, enjoyable, and inspiring.

Tips for creating usable navigational systems:

Navigation should...

- Be easy to learn.

- Be consistent throughout the website.

- Provide feedback, such as the use of breadcrumbs to indicate how to navigate back to where the user started.

- Use the minimum number of clicks to arrive at the next destination.

- Use clear and intuitive labels, based on the user's perspective and terminology.

- Support user tasks.

- Have each link be distinct from other links.

- Group navigation into logical units.

- Avoid making the user scroll to get to important navigation or submit buttons.

- Not disable the browser's back button.

OMG – Navigation is Unintuitive/Awful:

- [http://www.rentistoodamnhigh.org/]

- [http://www.leoburnett.ca/FLASH/index.htm]

- [http://www.cafeintl.net/] flash!

- [http://www.angelfire.com/super/badwebs/]

YES – Navigation is Intuitive and Easy to Use:

- [http://rzepak.pure.pl/] – non-English!

- [http://www.carbonica.org/]

- [http://www.getraenke-kukral.de/] – non-English too!

Navigation Testing:

We fully believe that any startup, that relies ONLY on the word of their web developer that the navigation used on their site works perfectly AND is the best practices examples – is looking to fail! You must test.....and you must get the testing done by experts!

Pay for testing at ~ Userlytics:

With Userlytics, you don't have to wait until a site, landing page, or display ad goes live before you know how the target will interact with it. Validate your concept by testing sketches; assure your functionality by testing wireframes; fine tune your design by testing prototypes; choose the best from your creative directions; and catch any last minute glitches by testing your final site, landing page and display ad before you start investing in multivariate analysis. [http://www.userlytics.com/]

Pay for testing at ~ Analytics Design Group:

Analytic Design Group Inc. has developed a proprietary navigation testing tool (called Navtester) that allows them to use a 'design & test' methodology when developing information architectures. Navtester allows their testers to user-test proposed site structures remotely, using an iterative test cycle to test and then refine the structure, and by using real users of your site, they can be sure that the information structure will be superior. And because the test is online and takes only around 15 to 20 minutes, the participation rate for the test is very high for very little

cost (compared to other labour and scheduling intensive methods like card sorting).
[http://www.analyticdesigngroup.com/]

Resources & Testing URLS -

[http://www.smashingmagazine.com/2009/02/18/9-common-usability-blunders/]

[http://graphicdesign.about.com/od/effectivewebsites/a/web_navigation.htm]

[http://vandelaydesign.com/blog/design/photoshop-navigation-tutorials/]

[http://www.wilsonweb.com/design/follansbee-nav-bar.htm]

Content

Web content is the textual, visual or aural content that is encountered as part of the user experience on websites. It may include, among other things: text, images, sounds, videos and animations. In *Information Architecture for the World Wide Web*, Lou Rosenfeld and Peter Morville write, "We define content broadly as 'the stuff in your Web site. This may include documents, data, applications, e-services, images, audio and video files, personal Web pages, archived e-mail messages, and more. And we include future stuff as well as present stuff."

So...content....perhaps you may have heard about the new marketing catch-phrase..."**Content Marketing**"...or "the creation or sharing of content for the purpose of engaging current and potential consumer bases..."

It goes by many names...let's try to name them all. *Custom publishing, custom media, customer media, customer publishing, member media, private media, branded content, corporate media, corporate publishing, corporate journalism and branded media.*

Perhaps nothing says it better than content marketing. But what exactly is content marketing in my mind?

"Content marketing is a marketing technique of creating and distributing relevant and valuable content to attract, acquire, and engage a clearly defined and understood target audience - with the objective of driving profitable customer action."

In other words, a marketing strategy to bring business to your site!

So how can you attract a new audience to come find you? You need something bigger and more exciting than a cookie. You need a birthday cake. **And a very exciting birthday cake!**

In other words, a piece of content that's exciting, that feels special, and that tastes good. (It doesn't hurt if it also has a great headline.)

Not only that, it has to show your potential audience that you know your stuff and that you solve a worthwhile problem. Otherwise they might enjoy scarfing down your content, but they won't bother coming back for more.

White papers, special reports, extended tutorials, manifestos and viral video all make excellent birthday cakes. **Contrary to popular belief, you do want marketing messages in your birthday cake content.** But they have to be palatable, subtle messages. You're not closing sales here . . . the birthday cake is just the beginning of the conversation.

Raise questions. Poke around at pain points that you can address in later content. Tell stories that resolve objections. But be subtle about it. The purpose of this content is to get your audience into a receptive state of mind before they start hearing any overt sales messages from you.

Create interest and desire for what you have to offer, but don't talk too much (if at all) about how you're going to solve all your audience's problems and make their lives wonderful.

If your birthday cake is compelling enough, **your audience will stick around to find those answers.**

And, of course, how does your birthday cake get in front of a new audience? By being remarkable enough to share. If it's not good enough to link to, bookmark, re-tweet, and email friends about, it's not good enough. Keep working on it, or partner with a content expert who can create something exceptional for you. And later we'll show you how to SEO it too!

Resources & Testing URLS -

[http://www.clickz.com/clickz/column/2015807/geology-content-marketing-strategy]

[http://en.wikipedia.org/wiki/Web_content]

[http://www.youtube.com/watch?v=9s8EfpKjYno]

Images

Not all images are created equal.

The right image on a web page can capture attention, inform, and even persuade your site visitors to convert to become more than a lead....to become a client or customer.

The right image can communicate who you and your company are more quickly and powerfully than words alone can do.

The wrong image, however, can confuse, annoy, and even repel your visitors.

The wrong image can give your audience a negative impression of your product, service, or company that you may never have a chance to correct.

You must use the best you can afford to use to make this conversion.

Using images in your website can be tricky. Images can brighten your website or destroy it completely. Many people are skeptical about using images because of SEO and bandwidth issues. In this article, I will explain why the worry is unnecessary if images are used correctly and intelligently.

Pay particular attention to the effectiveness of photography when testing with users. Regardless of the context, users rarely fail to comment on or be influenced by photography when shopping online.

Educate and Inform --

"Tell me and I'll forget, but show me and I'll remember." Learning can be difficult, but supporting theory with visual stimuli can help us grasp complex concepts and confirm our understanding. Images are easy to remember; how often have you met a new person and found later that you could recall their face but not their name?

Tell a Story --

From an early age we are told stories, and we spend our lives telling stories to friends and families. We know that pictures are effective storytelling tools. Even in the news media, multimedia slideshows are produced to give life to news stories.

Highlight Innovation --

People have certain expectations of how things should look and function. If you have a product that differs from the norm, expect a large portion of interest to come from word of mouth; friends will show it to friends, who will show it to their friends, and so on.

Evoke an Emotional Response --

Photography is often used to communicate hard-hitting messages (about the environment or human suffering, for example) because it evokes strong emotions. Charity campaigns, for example, know that by photography can get them the type of reaction they want.

Sell a Lifestyle --

Whether it's rural life, the good life or city living, everyone strives to live what they believe to be their perfect lifestyle, and we buy things that match that lifestyle. So, when products are displayed in the context of a lifestyle, we assign value to the product based on our desires.

Conclusion --

Photographs play a crucial role in informing, influencing, educating and reassuring customers throughout the buying process. Review your website's photography and question its role. What is the job of a particular photo at that particular stage of the process? Is it effective? When might customers drop out, and how could photos prevent that from happening?

The task of image selection often falls to the designer. User experience professionals should actively influence the process of selecting photos for the buying process.

The days of having a placeholder for images in our wireframes and prototypes are over. We should be annotating our work to influence decisions that art directors make when selecting images. Consider these principles to ensure that the images you choose not only "look right" but also work well.

Website owners should recall the principles mentioned in this article when commissioning new photos and researching stock. Focus on the purpose of the images, and you will turn photos from window dressing into key conversion tools.

Appropriateness

A good image captures attention, conveys emotion and tells a story. An image can make a webpage really effective not only because of its quality as mentioned, but also how well it fits into the context of the page. For example, it would not be appropriate to use black and white images if your site is about web hosting. Black and white images might work if you use it in an artistic site.

Technical Issues

There are 3 commonly used image formats in the web today, "Gif", "Jpeg" and "Png". As we want the image size to be as small as possible, the choice of using the different formats becomes critical. Gifs are more suitable for images with lesser colors while jpegs are more suitable for images with a great range of colors, for example, real life images. The size of jpeg images can be very small when compressed. Many photo editing software apps now a days have a "save for web" feature which can compress jpegs efficiently. Gifs on the other hand are very effective when used as transparent overlays. However, the quality of Gif overlays is not good. Pngs can produce very high quality images or transparent overlays but the tradeoff is their large file size.

Aesthetics

Effective images need to have a focus. Except when striving for a particular effect, fuzzy, vague or blurry pictures look unprofessional. There should also not be too many elements in an image because it distracts the reader from knowing what the image is about.

A balance of contrast and brightness is also important. Contrast is important to make your main character in the image stand out. For example, if you have a lady in green standing in front of a forest, the lady will not stand out because of the green. If you are using a black and white image, not enough contrast makes the entire image seem gray and washed out. The image should also not look too dark nor too bright, regardless of the subject matter.

Occasionally, you might wish to intentionally add a special effect on your image to create a dramatic effect. Silhouetting an image can achieve eye-popping results for a minimum amount of time and money. Ready-made filters and special add-on modules produce startling effect at a touch of a button. Shadows and gradients can give an image, button or icon a 3d effect which often makes it stand out prominently in your site. Using special effects can be tricky because your image will cease to be special if the effect is used too frequently. One typical example is the use of shadows and gradients. Many websites are using it so much so that the readers are focusing more on the graphics rather than the content. You need to save your best tricks for occasions that warrant them. In the worst scenario, people might be pissed off because of the images used in your website.

Cropping is one of the most powerful tool for improving the quality and impact of images. Cropping an image trims away unwanted elements and let you present the reader with only the most important part of the image. A good crop heightens the message, impact, and attractiveness of any image.

Lines of Action

Each image has its own internal geometry which can influence the look and feel of a webpage. Imagine every image you use is telling a story. Like arrows, images can lead your reader where to focus in your page. For example, if a person in the image is looking or gesturing in a certain direction, the reader's eyes will want to follow that gesture. People are very used to horizontal and vertical lines. Unless your site about design or creativity, you want the lines of action in your images to be horizontal or vertical as well. For example if you have straight objects like flag poles or tall buildings in your image, you want to make sure that they are aligned.

Layout

Placing images in different areas of your website can have different effect on the reader. Dominant images tell readers where to look at first and there should only be one dominant image in every page. All images used in a page need to spread out in a balanced way and be placed near to its relevant content. The spacing around each images is important. Like words, images need to breath as well. Too many images cluttering together can have an adverse effect on the reader. Running several images with a common theme close to each other, and with sufficient space can impart a sense of movement and guide the reader's eye to read the content.

Conclusion

An image can convey a lot more to the reader than a full page of text and is paramount if you want to the reader to believe in you. However, you have to be very careful of the image size and format to use, i.e. "Gif", "Jpeg" or "Png". Big image size over 50k can piss off dialup users easily. Page elements that draw the most attention also repel the most attention if used inappropriately.

OMG – Image Use is Awful:

- [http://www.gmlc-mcrn.org.uk/index.php?id=6] sizing!

- [http://lbrandy.com/blog/2008/10/my-first-and-last-webcomic/]

- [http://www.useit.com/alertbox/photo-content.html]

YES – Great Image Use:

- [http://www.mathieuclauss.com/] – non-English

- [http://www.seobook.com/blog]

- [http://www.polargold.de/]

Resources & Testing URLS -

[http://www.goodsignal.com/3-mistakes-to-avoid-with-website-images/]

[http://www.smashingmagazine.com/2010/06/25/how-to-use-photos-to-sell-more-online/]

[http://www.myapheus.com/escape-from-bad-web-design/]

Bonus to Your Users:

Documents/White Papers/PDFs

The benefits of this online marketing strategy translate directly into offline benefits as well. Clients who download the documents for viewing later on may also print them out. These documents are sometimes left lying around or presented at meetings. This attracts the attention of those who may not have been exposed to the product or service previously! The PDF documents might also be reproduced and distributed, creating a viral marketing effect.

[http://en.wikipedia.org/wiki/White_paper]

[http://www.searchmarketingstandard.com/optimise-pdf-files]

[http://www.wdfm.com/marketing-tips/white-paper.php]

1.2 – Products & Services

Offers...

When you sell services or Web apps online, you should do exactly the same thing that a store does: **show the product**. It's surprising how many websites that sell software for example, don't actually show screenshots of their applications. Sure, these are intangible goods, digital goods that you can't touch or smell, but they're still goods you can *see*.

Producing your own products boils down to 3 simple steps:

- plan it

- produce it

- and sell it

Create a marketing plan and complete your daily tasks. Not only will you eliminate procrastination, but you will give your product the best chance of success.

People make judgments based on what products look like.

Why? Because appearance is an indicator, rightly or wrongly, of a product's usability. This is known as the aesthetic-usability effect. If people see a complicated and cluttered interface or, in some cases, even just an unattractive interface, they may assume it is not very usable or is hard to learn. On the other hand, if people see an attractive and simple-looking interface, they may start figuring out how it works right then and will want to give it a try. Get people to imagine using your software, and you'll get closer to closing the sale. Get people to run a trial for your software and those conversions will rise dramatically!

Define Your USP...
Before spending a single moment designing your online advertising campaigns, your company needs to decide on its unique selling proposition or "USP." A company's USP is the one compelling selling point of your organization that sets you apart from the competition. Are you the fastest, highest quality, or least expensive option? Does your team have any exceptionally unique credentials?

Find Where Your Target Market Is Looking...
If you've been reading about different Internet marketing strategies, you've probably seen a lot of hype about how "pay-per-click," or "media buying," or any number of other online channels is the best way to go. The truth is, not all Internet searchers look in the same places, and each strategy can be effective if you are targeting the right people.

The first step to determining where your efforts are best focused is to determine if your product is something people are actively searching for. Google's keyword tool is an excellent free tool for figuring this out. Simply type in words or phrases that are closely related to your product and Google will tell you how many people search for those things monthly.

If your product is not something that is heavily searched for, it does not mean that you cannot successfully sell it online. Instead, it might mean that you offer something original that few people have thought to search for. In this case, you must think about the kind of websites your audience might be reading and deliver your marketing there.

Write/Design Effective Product Showcases....
Now that you've thought a bit more about where the bulk of your marketing efforts belong, it's time to write/design Product copy that gets people to your website **and sells your product.** Think back to your USP and center the focus of your marketing around it. Remember, your USP is what sets you apart from all of your competitors, which means that without one your ad will not stand out from the rest in any special way....i.e. **use outbound product marketing to create buzz...**

Most web surfers are good at tuning out everything that isn't directly applicable to them. Because of this, your ads and website copy cannot be all about you. Starting off your copy by talking about how long you've been in business, how decorated your team is, or how innovative you think you are, is a bad approach because it has nothing to do with the customer and does not demonstrate an understanding of their problem. Instead, strive to make an emotional connection through your USP and communicate that you know what they're feeling and how to help them.

Market your products...all the rest is futile!

3M's "open up this unbreakable glass case and the $100,000 is yours" marketing challenge!

[http://en.wikipedia.org/wiki/Product_marketingg]

[http://www.bestdesigntuts.com/creative-design-incredible-way-of-product-marketing/]

[http://internetmarketingstrategiesinfo.com/articles/why-produce-your-own-products-to-increase-sales]

Sales...

Selling your own products online is what any website is doing via its chance to impress its website visitors. If you have a know-how or expertise that no one else has, you may certainly sell that through your website.

Costs for selling online are really low in dollars but expensive in time-spent – you only have to maintain your website alive and put relevant content about your product on that site.

Thanks to the Internet and your website, you have access to millions of people all over the world who actively search the net for anything new and interesting. It is also a well-known fact that consumers are more prone to spend money online, from the convenience of their homes.

Why not take advantage of all these favorable circumstances and start selling your own product, service, book, or anything else you wish?

Even passive income can be a beneficial way to create time to spend on other pursuits....

[http://www.businessknowhow.com/marketing/]

[http://www.practicalecommerce.com/articles/267-What-Should-I-Sell-Online-]

[http://store.yahoo.com/how-to-sell-online.html]

1.3 – Call to Actions

The term "call to action" means, well, just what it sounds like – **it's instructing someone to do what you want them to do, or calling them to action.**

For example, a successful call to action can motivate a customer to click on a link at the end of a blog post, reply to an e-mail, or "like" your post on Facebook. After your readers have finished reading your content, a call to action provides web visitors with the next step, leading them one step closer to converting from a visitor to a customer. **Whether it's completing a sale or downloading an article, a strong call to action is an important part of any marketing strategy – perhaps it's said the MOST important part of any strategy!**

Why is a Call to Action Important?
A call to action forces participation from a reader, either in the form of leaving a comment, sending a re-tweet, and so on. Some readers may only comment if they are told to comment, so a strong call to action encourages readers that it's ok to share their thoughts. A call to action motivates people to respond to a post that they know the solution to or have a strong opinion about. When people see that others have understood the call to action and are

expressing their opinions, they are more likely to do, as they know the site is trusted and fun to participate in.

How to Write a Call to Action

When writing your own call to action, it is important to **keep things quick and simple with the addition of a question or comment**. This way, people are not discouraged or confused by how to respond. The call to action should not take up a great deal of time or require instruction, as users should be able to easily respond without any confusion. **Make your call to action obvious; let your users know exactly what you are asking of them.**

Call to Action Techniques

When creating your own call to action, remember to keep it simple. It is important to make it obvious what you are asking the reader to do and make it clear where the call to action is.

Your call to action should also be obtainable, as **the simpler it is the more likely that people will participate.**

Your call to action **should stand out**, and encourage readers to interact with your article or website.

It is also helpful to **put the call to action in bold or even use a different font or a quote bo**x so that it will stand out and look different from the rest of the text.

A call to action is also effective when it is **urgent**, and demands the readers to do what you want, when you want them to do it. Using phrases like "**buy now**", or "**click here**", encourages readers to respond immediately

Writing calls-to-action

Using the right words appropriate to your website will drive people to take the action; using the wrong words can distract them, at best, or cause them to leave your website, at worst. With that in mind, here are some tips for writing effective calls-to-action:

•Lay the groundwork – Before someone is willing to follow one of your calls-to-action, they first have to recognize a need that requires them doing so. Telling your visitors the benefits of taking that action will help give them the motivation to actually do so.

•Use action-oriented words – Using an active voice encourages people to follow your calls-to-action, and also helps people scanning your website quickly identify what your call-to-action is about. This is also one of the reasons you should avoid using "click here" in your link text.

•Have one on every page – There should always be at least one call-to-action within the content on every page of your website – no page should be a dead-end. Ending your content with a call-to-action tells visitors what the next step is and keeps them moving on your website.

•Limit the number and keep them distinct – Having too many calls-to-action on a website can be confusing for your visitors. Limit yourself to only a few, and keep them distinct so visitors know what the primary call-to-action is, as well as what you want them to do first from the choices.

•Keep your forms short and clear – Unless someone has a compelling interest, many people see a long form asking for unnecessary information and won't fill it out. Follow some of my other tips for writing clear instructions if your main call-to-action is a form.

Designing calls-to-action

Web designers can have a lot of influence over how effective calls-to-action are. Following general usability and design guidelines help make the website as effective as possible. Here are some tips for how to do that:

•Put it above the fold – You want your main call-to-action to be visible wherever people go throughout your website – almost like your logo. The right side of your website's header is a natural location to do that; any other lesser calls-to-action can go in sidebars, above the fold as well.

•Use images for emphasis – Images or icons get people's attention because they get noticed by your eyes before content on a page does. Buttons also do the same thing and are great to use because they stand out against text AND imply action by their very nature.

•Choose contrasting colors – If you're using a button as your primary call-to-action mechanism, use a color that contrasts with your main colors for maximum effect. Just don't choose a color that contrasts so much that it becomes too hard to ignore when reading the content around it.

•Consider homepage placement – We all know how important your homepage is, which is why you need to make it as usable as possible for your visitors. Your main call-to-action should be prominently placed on it where people will really see it.

•Use some white space – The more white space around your call-to-action, the more people's eyes will naturally be drawn to it. Crowding your call-to-action in with surrounding content will decrease its effectiveness as it gets lost in the overall noise of the page.

•Make it bigger – Size isn't everything when it comes to your call-to-action, but making it bigger definitely makes it more likely that it will get noticed. Just don't make it so big that it totally overwhelms the rest of the content on your website – find the right balance.

The Color Of Call-To-Action

COLOR	NATURE OF ASSOCIATIONS	WHERE TO USE	DRAWBACKS
Red	increases your heart rate by activating your pituitary gland	a classic call to action color	might be associated with *debt and danger*
Yellow	the first color a person sees	**draw attention** to your call-to-action	
Orange	combination of aggressive red and cheerful yellow	perfect call-to-action	
Blue			may make your visitor *reconsider* the action
Green	the easiest for the eyes	good for testimonials, founder's story, etc	
White	gives other colors prominence	make your call-to-action **stand out**	

The following **best practices** should be applied to calls to action (C2A) that you create to entice visitors to click through to your offer page (landing page) and convert into a lead.

- Action-oriented. Start with a verb and tell the visitor what action to take.
- Positive. Stress the benefits to the visitor.
- Clear. Indicates exactly what action to take, and/or the result of that action.
- Direct. Brief. To the point. Focused.
- Have both a primary and a secondary call to action

- Placement "above the fold"--in the top section of the page--so that your forms are visible to viewers without scrolling
- Be highlighted with color or graphics to draw attention.
- Placed on multiple pages of your site, not just the homepage or a landing page.

[http://www.canuckseo.com/index.php/2011/01/seo-marketing-make-a-call-to-action/]

[http://designshack.co.uk/articles/inspiration/25-examples-of-convincing-call-to-action-buttons]

[http://www.hongkiat.com/blog/call-to-action-buttons-guidelines-best-practices-and-examples/]

Resources & Testing URLS -

[http://visualwebsiteoptimizer.com/split-testing-blog/tag/call-to-action-split-testing/]

[http://visualwebsiteoptimizer.com/split-testing-blog/guess-the-ab-test-winner/]

[http://www.koozai.com/blog/search-marketing/website-testing-opportunity-2-call-to-action-button/]

Call to Action Collaterals...

Testimonials...

When done right, testimonials can be a strong ally in establishing the credibility of your website. When done wrong, they can actually do more harm than good. I'm sure you've seen websites loaded with testimonials that all sound as though they were written by the same bad advertising copywriter. Breathless, urgent, loaded with supposedly "hypnotic" sales trigger words - and completely unbelievable. Nothing will ruin your credibility faster than the use of phony testimonials. It's perfectly okay to solicit testimonials. Ask your customers for feedback, and include the best comments on your website. However, do not under any circumstances succumb to the temptation to write your own testimonials or to hire someone to write them for you.

[http://superbadinternetmarketing.com/what-you-need-to-know-about-endorsements-and-testimonials-on-your-website/]

[http://www.allbusiness.com/company-activities-management/sales-selling/14435321-1.html]

[http://www.canuckseo.com/index.php/2011/01/seo-marketing-make-a-call-to-action/]

Reviews...

Many people think that reliable web hosting reviews are important for people to get the help in the web hosting world. In fact, getting the reliable web hosting reviews has become something difficult in recent years. You could see that there are numerous web hosting companies established in the world nowadays. And the number of web hosting service providers in the market would continue to increase in the future.

A study conducted by eVOC and RelevantView shows that 89+% of shoppers are more likely to make a contact or purchase at sites that offer generated reviews.

Similarly, an independent study done by Superpages.com shows that businesses with a rating or review receive double the performance (in clicks / contacts) of listings without.

A ComScore/Kelsey Group study found that 24% of users who purchase local services (such as restaurants and hotels) consult online reviews before making a decision. Research from the e-tailing group shows that 53% of consumers using ratings and reviews are doing this so they can decide between businesses that they are considering to purchase from. 28% said that they used reviews and ratings to confirm that they made the right decision in choosing a particular business. Reviews count, period.

[http://blog.imprezziomarketing.com/index.php/google-maps/the-importance-of-reviews-on-google-maps/]

[http://www.dreamsystemsmedia.com/blog/index.php/
how-to-get-yelp-reviews/]

RECAP: 1-click Best Practices tactics to make that offer!
Okay, this is so basic in Marketing 101 that I'm always a bit
taken back by new clients, who have never learned that if
you want business from website visitors, you need to ASK
for it! Yup, that's still one of the most necessary items in
any website's marketing strategy; the "call-to-action" must
be present, eh! And what is same, you might ask...ah....let
me explain! A "call-to-action" is a button of any size,
shape, color or design that is there for the website visitor –
your prospective new client/customer to click on, to begin
the process of turning that "lead" into a new
client/customer. It's that easy and it's that difficult all at
the same time, and here's why in a nutshell.

[http://www.smashingmagazine.com/2009/04/06/desig
n-to-sell-12-tips-to-help-your-website-convert/]

[http://www.smashingmagazine.com/2009/05/05/optim
izing-improvig-conversion-rates-less-effort-more-
customers/]

[http://www.smashingmagazine.com/2009/10/13/call-
to-action-buttons-examples-and-best-practices/]

[http://www.smashingmagazine.com/2009/05/23/optim
izing-conversion-rates-less-effort-more-customers/]

1.4 – Conversion Tracking

A/B and/or Multivariate Testing...
The attention span on the Web has been decreasing ever since Google had arrived and changed the rules of the game. Now with millions of results available on any topic imaginable, the window to grab a visitor's attention has decreased significantly (in 2002, the BBC reported it is about 9 seconds).

Picture yourself browsing the Web: do you go out of your way to read the text, look at all the graphics, and try to thoroughly understand what the page is about? The answer is most likely to be a straight "no."

With bombardment of information from all around, we have become spoiled kids, not paying enough attention to what a Web page wants to tell us. We make snap decisions on whether to engage with a website based on whatever we can make out in the first few milliseconds.

The responsibility for making a good first impression lies with designers and website owners. Given that the window of opportunity to persuade a visitor is really small, most designs (probably including yours) do a sub-optimal job because the designer in you thinks in terms of aesthetics.

However, most websites do not exist just to impress visitors.

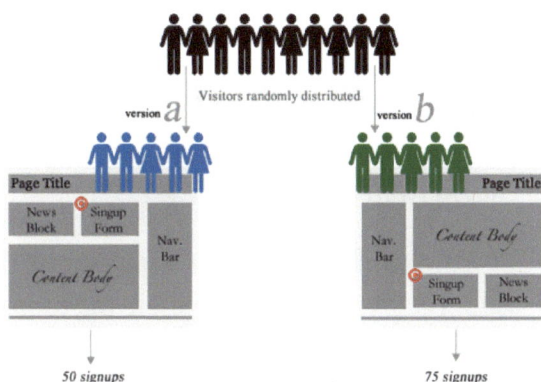

Version B is better than version A

Most websites exist to turn a prospective lead into a client or customer via your sales funnel. Whether it is to get visitors to subscribe to the blog feed, or to download a trial, every website ultimately exists to make a sale of some kind.

Remember….hypothesize….test….analyze…

then retest…..

[http://www.smashingmagazine.com/2010/11/24/multivariate-testing-in-action-five-simple-steps-to-increase-conversion-rates/]

[http://20bits.com/articles/an-introduction-to-ab-testing/]

Analytics & Statistics...

Google Analytics is undoubtedly the most widely used web analytics application. Emerged from and based upon the analytics-package developed by Urchin Software Corporation (which was bought by Google in April 2005), the tool has become publicly available for free under the new flagship of Google Analytics.

In May 2007 the application was heavily edited, developed and released; the design was simplified and more advanced featured were added. Over years Google Analytics managed to gain on popularity because of its simplicity and many advanced features for curious site owners and professional marketers.

We will not go into same here as you all most likely have a Google account and already track your traffic, site stats etc...

[http://www.smashingmagazine.com/2009/07/16/a-guide-to-google-analytics-and-useful-tools/]

[http://fivesecondtest.com/]

[http://en.wikipedia.org/wiki/Web_analytics]

[http://www.seomoz.org/ugc/the-clickthrough-the-lead-capture-and-the-infommercial]

[http://www.bazaarvoice.com/resources/stats]

WEEKLY TASKS

2.0 Weekly SEO Foundation Tasks

Search engine optimization (SEO) is the research-based approach of improving the volume and quality of traffic to a web site from search engines via "natural" ("organic" or "algorithmic") search results. Search engine optimization targets the **free, organic, natural, or left hand side of search and** their ranking algorithms. Differing from a pay-per-click (PPC) advertising program such as Google Adwords, the organic listings targeted by search engine optimization cannot be manipulated by paying a fee for favorable placement. Web sites which rank on the first page of search engine results are scored based on a wide array of very specific criteria, the secrets of which search engines guard very closely. For this reason, effective search engine optimization is the only way to gain a top placement among the free or natural search engine listings.

With over 3.7 BILLION searches conducted each day, search engines are the most widely used method of attracting traffic to a web site — with research confirming that over 90% of prospective web customers use search engines to find solutions and vendors. Furthermore, only the top 10 search results will generate a majority of search traffic and subsequent conversions. It will not benefit a company or its products to rank below the first page of natural search engine results.

It is very important to understand that the search engines read only the text content of pages; there is no way for them to read graphics, therefore the words used in the text of web pages is **critically** important to that site's ranking. The key determinant in how various pages rank in internet searches has to do with the sophisticated algorithms used by search engine databases to determine the relevancy of a page to the word or words that are being searched for...or **your keywords!**

There are a number factors that are evaluated by these programs which vary from one search engine company to another and are subject to constant change and revision. Some of the consistent factors in relevancy ranking on a given keyword or phrases include the following:

- **The frequency of the keyword within the text of the page.**
- **The use of the keyword in important places within the page, such as the page title, a headline, in an image name or a hyperlink.**
- **The percentage of that keyword's use when compared to the total number of words on the page...NSI now....**
- **The number of links to that page from other sites on the internet.**
- **The authority/trust level of those referring IBL sites...**

2.1 – Keyword Research

Wikipedia – Search Engine Optimization

First, you will need to attempt to define your Keyword phrases for your products or services; discover your competitor's usage of their own keywords; develop a completely new set of keyword candidates for your own use and then re subscribe to the top 10 search engines.

One must develop your original set of keyword phrases for broad and exact keywords chosen and they will all have to be "phrased" for your use, before one can actually begin to test them as they are and that newly phrased keyword list will become the benchmark for your keyword positioning strategy.

You will also have to first, check that all keyword terms are being used properly and that each term exists, or will have to be re-phrased and that any 'extra' terms be listed but only as 'alternates' to your original list.

Here's a quick look at the basics in an Infographic that I use to try to explain how to formulate a keyword research plan….

[http://www.canuckseo.com/index.php/2010/12/keywords-101this-great-infographic-shows-all/]

From SEOmoz…they rationalize the process as follows….

Ask yourself…

Is the keyword relevant to the content your website offers? Will searchers who find your site through this term find the likely answer to their implied question(s)? And will this traffic result in financial rewards (or other organizational goals) directly or indirectly? If the answer to all of these questions is a clear "Yes!" then proceed...

Search for the term/phrase in the major engines…
Are there search advertisements running along the top and right-hand side of the organic results? Typically, many search ads means a high value keyword, and multiple search ads above the organic results often means a highly lucrative and directly conversion-prone keyword.

Buy a sample campaign…
For the keyword at Google AdWords and/or Bing AdCenter and then for example in Google Adwords, choose "exact match" and point the traffic to the most relevant page on your website. Measure the traffic to your site, and track impressions and conversion rate over the course of at least 2-300 clicks (this may take only a day or two with highly trafficked terms, or several weeks with keywords in lesser demand).

Using the data you've collected…
Make an educated guess about the value of a single visitor to your site with the given search term or phrase. For

example, if, in the past 24 hours, your search ad has generated 5,000 impressions, of which 100 visitors have come to your site and 3 have converted for total profit (not revenue!) of $300, then a single visitor for that keyword is worth approx. $3 to your business. Those 5,000 impressions in 24 hours could probably generate a click-through rate of between 30-40% with a #1 ranking which would mean 1500-2000 visits per day, at $3 each, or ~$1.75 million dollars per year. No wonder businesses love search marketing!

[http://www.seomoz.org/beginners-guide-to-seo/keyword-research]

[http://www.seomoz.org/article/keyword-research-guide]

[http://pro.seomoz.org/tools/on-page-keyword-optimization]

2.2 – On-Page Optimization

You will need to use the original re-phrased keyword set as the base set for use in each website page's "on-page" SEO. By this term you will need to understand all of the variables that exist on each of your <HTML> pages that will need to be modified – your <head> tags area, the <title> tag, the <body> contents text blocks, your <image> tags and their <alt> modifiers, your <header> and <footer> links, all on-page URLS and all interior navigational links and URLs too.

This is a very detailed job that requires much knowledge of the "best practices" that are most current so that you will entail no search engine penalties for your website.

Here is a short list of some of the basic items that you will need to work on, for your on-page optimization basics...

[http://www.canuckseo.com/index.php/2009/11/diy-canadian-seo-chapter-1/]

[http://www.canuckseo.com/index.php/2009/11/diy-canadian-seo-chapter-2/]

[http://www.canuckseo.com/index.php/2009/12/diy-canadian-seo-chapter-3/]

[http://www.canuckseo.com/index.php/2010/02/diy-canadian-seo-google-local-maps/]

[http://www.seomoz.org/learn-seo/on-page-factors]

[http://www.canuckseo.com/index.php/2010/03/home-pages-must-rule/]

[http://www.canuckseo.com/index.php/2010/04/an-un-scheduled-seo-potpourri/]

[http://www.canuckseo.com/index.php/2010/05/diy-canadian-seo-chapter-4/]

[http://www.canuckseo.com/index.php/2010/08/diy-canadian-seo-chapter-5/]

[http://www.seomoz.org/ugc/using-on-page-techniques-to-leverage-your-off-page-seo]

[http://www.canuckseo.com/index.php/2010/11/diy-canadian-seo-google-placesearch-you/]

On Page – Titles…

Google uses only up to 56/58 chars. for the <title> tag – well, it stores more than that in its index, but will show "usually" up to only the first 56 or so of same.

How do I know? Best practices from most if not all of the SEO community say so….Google for it and you'll see….

Keywords are what we use…to "salt" the <title> tag with same so that when Google indexes that page, those keywords are used by Google to "rank" that page.

Here's my own 57 char <title> tag for my CanuckSEO blog home page –

<title>Canadian SEO | Local Canadian SEO | Hamilton SEO|kkti.com</title>

As you can see, you simply place your keywords, in descending order of importance for your page, from left to right.

But what about the name of the blog – my "brand" if you will…why is it last?

Simple, as it will rank on its own for that simple term ALWAYS highly placed within Google....there is no need to "lead" with the brand name....it should always follow last.

Let's look at some example <title> tags taken from a variety of pages....

- <title>Bomb Beverages - index</title>

- <title>ICE SYRUP - Pure Canadian Grape Syrup</title>

- <TITLE>MOWSSER ORTHOPAEDIC WRIST SUPPORT SYSTEM - CANADA</TITLE>

- <title>Services - THAAT</title>

- <title>Welcome to Gridco Ltd</title>

- <title>Welcome to indieOPTION - indieOPTION</title>

What's the char count for each and what 's wrong with each? ☺

And how important was <title> for SEO success? By the whole SEO community, it remains the #1 item to ensure that you optimize to get ranked!

[http://www.seomofo.com/snippet-optimizer.html]

2.3 – Off-Page Optimization

A large part of any SEO campaign is the ability to discern and develop your own specialized lists of authority sites, trusted sites, forums, search engines for you to list your website with in regards to acquire backlinks. These are truly "incoming" back links (**IBLs**) and you must remember that this has shown to be only one manner in which to achieve higher rankings without delving into the reciprocal exchanges in non-sector link farms and such items.

More than that is the realization that to build truly great incoming back links you will need to have the best – the most superb content on your website that you can develop yourself. It helps not for long, to succumb to the faulty tactic of "scraping" content from other sites and putting same on your own – Google has reported that such "scraper" sites will be devalued in their search engine rankings which everyone from content farms, major publishing houses, aggregator sites and all of the sites that either buy or sell links.

- **DIY Guide to Successful Linkbait [<u>Voltier Creative</u>]**

And yes you will need to include business social networking backlink candidates as well at many global social media sites too! You will hand submit personalized requests to all of your backlink website candidates for each and every one of them for your website to see the resulting climb in your website ranking positions as a result.

Checking rankings, making modifications, re-submitting the site and keeping an eye on competition for rankings is an ongoing process. Check your positions at least once a week and be aware of the rise and/or fall of the site's rank. Look at the sites above yours (and the sites with links to them) and try to determine what those sites are doing right. Also, examine your site traffic reports, which can tell you where your traffic is coming from and the keyword queries that brought those visitors to the site.

SEO Analytics Software ~
What follows here is a list of both software for running your own analytics or using a hosted service as well, to generate reliable serps (search engine ranking positional reports) on a paid for basis.

- [http://blog.diyseo.com/]
- [http://www.seomoz.com]
- [http://raventools.com/]
- [http://www.myseotool.com]
- [http://www.canuckseo.com/index.php/2011/02/new-for-canadian-seo-getlisted-org-comes-to-canada/]
- [http://www.canuckseo.com/index.php/2011/03/smbs-owning-your-own-web-equity/]

SEO Experts Who May Help Guide your Campaign ~
A short list of SEO practitioners who may often provide answers for you and your own SEO campaigns, if properly asked and may often provide that help on an ongoing basis! I know each of these folks and love what they do and they do very well for their own clients! Remember to become a daily visitor for their own blogs too!

Ross Hudgens ~ [http://www.rosshudgens.com/]

Andrew Shotland ~
[http://www.localseoguide.com]

David Mihm ~
[http://www.davidmihm.com/blog/]

Dev Basu ~ [http://www.poweredbysearch.com]

Rand Fishkin ~ [http://www.seomoz.org/blog]

Mark Murnahan ~ [http://www.awebguy.com/]

Mike Blumenthal ~
[http://blumenthals.com/blog/]

3.0 Daily Social Media Foundation Tasks

First some background on this strategy from Wikipedia on Social Media...

"Social media are media for social interaction, using highly accessible and scalable publishing techniques. Social media uses web-based technologies to turn communication into interactive dialogues.

"Social Media is a group of Internet-based applications that build on the ideological and technological foundations of Web 2.0, which allows the creation and exchange of user-generated content."

"Social authority is developed when an individual or organization establishes themselves as an "expert" in their given field or area, thereby becoming an "influencer" in that field or area."

http://en.wikipedia.org/wiki/Social_media

And a latest comScore survey results show that **39%** of all search engine users believe that "...seeing a company listed among the top search engine results make them think that the company is a leader in its field!"

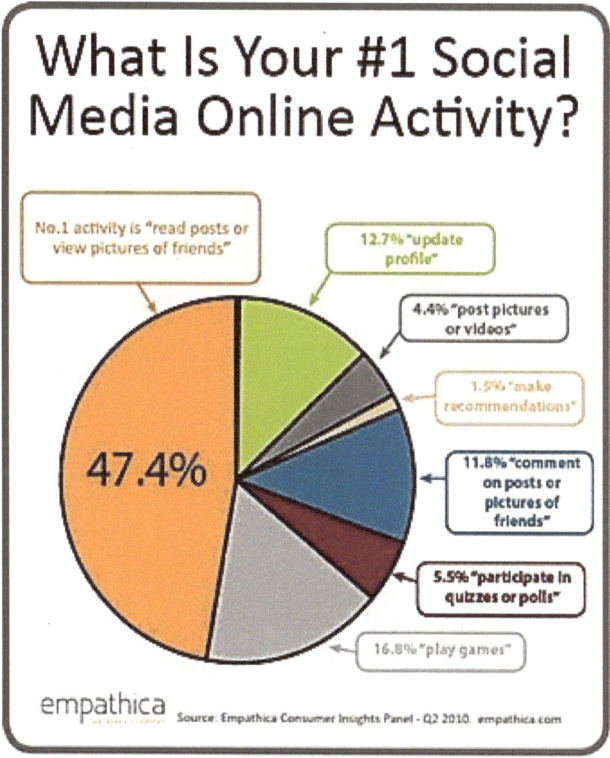

What Is Your #1 Social Media Online Activity?

No.1 activity is "read posts or view pictures of friends"

12.7% "update profile"

4.4% "post pictures or videos"

1.5% "make recommendations"

11.8% "comment on posts or pictures of friends"

5.5% "participate in quizzes or polls"

16.8% "play games"

47.4%

empathica

Source: Empathica Consumer Insights Panel - Q2 2010. empathica.com

Why is Social Media Important to me?

Look at this chart, from Empathica....almost half of the online world read posts or view pictures online...and only 1.5% of online folks "make recommendations!"

Imagine that...i.e. if your customers make recommendations about your business – about half of the online world may see it...

And learn about you and your products or services having the "mind-set" that your items are quality, trusted and reliable too!

Social media works!

Social media has become a part of daily life for many Internet users. Social media is primarily a venue for personal communication between individuals. However, many social media sites have evolved and people have found ways to use them for business purposes as well.

Sites such as Facebook, LinkedIn, and Twitter can be a great way to generate new business by using your existing network of friends.

Other sites such as social bookmarking sites (Digg, Delicious, etc.) can generate traffic to your website from articles that you post.

If an article posted on a major social bookmarking site receives enough bookmarks to be listed on the front page, it could generate thousands of visitors to your website...visitors who just may buy something!

Blogs and forums are other types of social media. These types of social media provide you with additional content posted by yourself and by your users, which will result in more traffic to your website as well as more brand coverage.

HubSpot Charts show this well....

Benefits of social media marketing

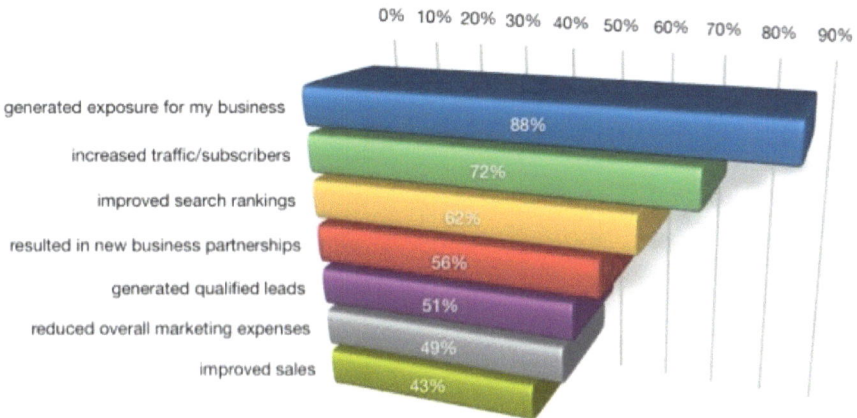

And HubSpot.com also has an excellent Online Marketing Blueprint .pdfs and a whole host of others too....

[http://www.hubspot.com/blueprint/]

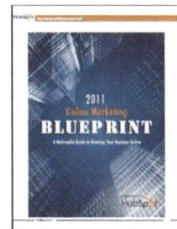

3.1 – Social Media Authority

What is Social Authority?

One of the key components in successful social media marketing implementation is building "social authority."

Social authority is developed when an individual or organization establishes themselves as an "expert" in their given field or area, thereby becoming an "influencer" in that field or area...

Why can that be important to SME business owners?

It is through this process of "building social authority" that social media becomes effective. That is why one of the foundational concepts in social media has become that you cannot completely control your message through social media but rather you can simply begin to participate in the "conversation" in the hopes that you can become a relevant influence in that conversation.

However, this conversation participation must be cleverly executed because while people are resistant to marketing in general, they are even more resistant to direct or overt marketing through social media platforms...

How to become a Social Authority?

Your conversation participation with prospective customers must be cleverly executed...because they are even more resistant to direct or overt marketing through social media platforms...

You cannot expect people to be receptive to a marketing message in and of itself....from social media outlets...as your prospects most trusted company or product information coming from "people like me" -- inferred to be information from someone they trusted...

So to become an Authority, you need to establish **TRUST** and **CREDIBLE** Authority to your marketplace....

So the Rationale in trying to become a Social Media Authority is...

Someone performing a "marketing" role within a company must ***honestly*** convince people of their ***genuine*** intentions, knowledge, and expertise in a specific area or industry through providing valuable and accurate information on an ongoing basis without a marketing angle overtly associated...

If this can be done, trust with, and of, the recipient of that information – and that message itself – begins to develop naturally. This person or organization becomes a thought leader and value provider - setting themselves up as a trusted ***advisor*** instead of marketer.

RECOMMENDATIONS VIA
SOCIAL MEDIA DRIVE
OFFLINE BEHAVIOR

38% of consumers have
followed through (at least once)
with a friend's recommendation they
have received via social media

empathica   Source: Empathica Consumer Insights Panel - Q2 2010. empathica.com

Top of mind awareness develops and the consumer naturally begins to gravitate to the products and/or offerings of the authority/influencer…**by protecting your company name!**

Why would being a Social Media Authority be a good way to help build website traffic to your website?

- 38% or more than 1 in every 3 of us, reads via social media a recommendation or referral from a friend — and then follow thru on same! [Empathica.com Report]

- 56% of online businesses spend more than 6 hours weekly on social media marketing? And of that number, 12% of them spend more than 20 hours weekly?

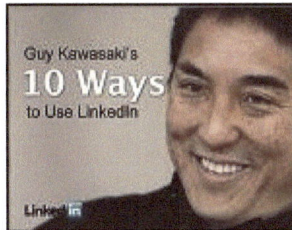

- [http://www.flowtown.com/blog/everybodys-doing-it-how-marketers-are-utilizing-social-media-in-2010?display=wide]

- Use LinkedIN to get new Targeted Biz Traffic! [CanuckSEO.com]

- Where Social and Rank Meet... [Blumenthals.com/blog]

- Social Media Reality Check [Newswire.ca]

- Infographics for Social Media Understanding [http://searchengineland.com/7-local-web-marketing-infographics-to-overload-your-brain-68444]

- **Lee Odden on Social Media**
  [http://www.toprankblog.com/2011/03/integrate
  d-seo-social-media/]

- **SEOMoz on Social Media Authority and Influence**
  [http://www.seomoz.org/ugc/social-authority-meets-
  search-measuring-influence]

Note the common Venn items…….FaceBook, Twitter, LinkedIn and Skype!

3.2 – Social Media Community

Social Media Authority, leads to positioning that one can expect will lead to the following increase in awareness on the web...i.e. the formation of your own Social Media Community...

People Streams

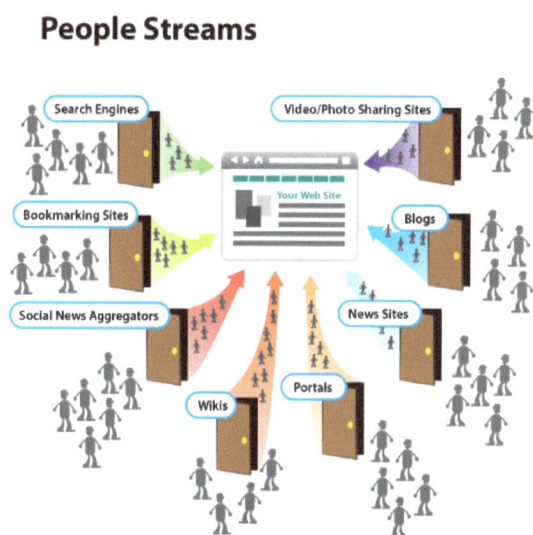

Social Media Communities are built via the generation of links, i.e. backlinks from relevant sites and the more links from authority sites, the more people view the linked to author's content as authoritative.

All the while, your increased links lead to increased ranking in Google and Bing/Yahoo and many people take high rankings in search engines to mean that Google itself has decided that the site is yes, an Authority.

And remember, that search has higher conversion rates than most other media, which means it is viewed less as advertising and more as trusted referrals.

Authority gives birth to Community!

Building your new Social Community, means helping forge more online friends/followers /Likes from other social media sites too like portals, wikis, blogs, photo gallery sites too... all through outright networking, than necessarily via content. Once again, the more friends/fans/Likes someone has, the more they are viewed as an authority, and the more likely they are to have others view their work and opinions as authoritative. **Yes, Social Authority builds Community!**

Tactical methods to enable your own Social Media Authority....

- **Blogs ~** [http://www.socialmediaexaminer.com/26-ways-to-use-social-media-for-lead-generation/#more-8364]

- **Email Marketing ~** [http://www.clickz.com/clickz/column/2032325/email-social]

- [http://www.openforum.com/idea-hub/topics/marketing/article/start-somewhere-with-social-media-chris-brogan]

- **Speaking Engagements ~** [http://lesliealbritton.com/marketing-your-brand-through-speaking-engagements.shtml]

- **Article Writing ~**
  [http://ezinearticles.com/?Website-and-Blog-Traffic---How-Does-Article-Marketing-Help?&id=4906076]

- **Facebook ~**
  [http://www.facebook.com/topic.php?uid=59400547335&topic=8866]
  [http://www.insidefacebook.com/2007/12/09/inside-facebook-marketing-bible-24-ways-to-market-your-brand-company-product-or-service-in-facebook/]

- **LinkedIN ~**
  [http://linkedinformarketing.com/]
  [http://www.pamorama.net/2010/03/29/how-to-use-linkedin-to-market-your-business/]

- **Twitter ~**
  [http://www.allentan.net/blog/2011/02/18/how-twitter-marketing-can-help-your-business/]
  [http://blog.hubspot.com/blog/tabid/6307/bid/7178/Twitter-Rolls-Out-Analytics-Tool.aspx]
  [http://www.ehow.com/how_6887833_develop-effective-twitter-marketing-strategies.html]

- **Google News Alerts ~**
  [http://www.google.com/support/alerts/bin/static.py?hl=en&page=guide.cs&guide=28413&rd=1]
  [http://www.makeuseof.com/tag/5-interesting-ways-google-news-rss-feeds/]

- **Social Media Analytics ~**
  [http://www.toprankblog.com/2010/03/11-free-tools-for-social-media-optimization/]

[http://www.socialmediaexaminer.com/26-ways-to-use-social-media-for-lead-generation/#more-8364]
[http://www.slideshare.net/kunocreative/presentations]
[http://www.optify.net/internet-marketing/optify-resources/]

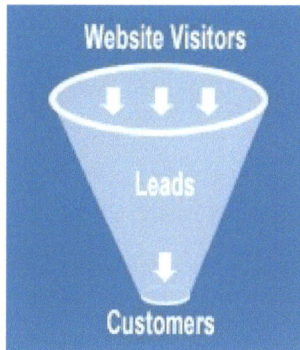

4.0 Monitoring & Analytics Tasks

Once you have the basics "in hand," that is you've at least begun the tasks that we've scheduled for you in this marketing program, you will find that the most stringent of tasks – monitoring those tasks, is still to come.

You will need tools to do this and while we've listed some of them here below, you must remember that no matter how you much data you get, you need to constantly look at that data to get the information that you can use – to tweak and change and modify all of the other factors already in place.

You will need to monitor all of the various aspects of the sales process, and yes, you will also need to tweak your Sales Conversions too. Basically, your Sales Conversion funnel breaks down into 4 main areas…

1. **Create an offer**

2. **Build a call to action**

3. **Build a landing page**

4. **Measure, test and then tweak....**

The Sales Funnel metaphor has its roots in the real world use of funnels. A large amount of liquid, or website visitors, can fit into the top wide portion of the funnel. However, as you move down toward the funnel neck, less and less opportunities can fit as those visitors thin and leave less numbers of leads. Finally those leads turn into customers, at the bottom end of the funnel and that means that you made e and offer where two parties exchange something of value.

 On the chance that you might not know at any given moment exactly what your online marketing program has produced revenue stream wise – you would be wise to remember that unless you check these numbers daily, you will never know for sure!

You will of course need analytics to show you just what kind of traffic your site is receiving, what kind of conversions you're achieving, what kind of bounce rates and click-thrus are occurring and finally, what kind of revenues you receive.

So here's a short list of various sites that you can look over to check out what types of analytics are "out there" and most have a free or free trial period for same.

- http://www.google.com/analytics
- http://sitescanga.com/
- http://yoast.com/out/clicky/
- http://www.clicktale.com/
- http://www.google.com/websiteoptimizer
- https://www.google.com/webmasters/tools/home?hl=en
- https://www.google.com/webmasters/tools/home?hl=en
- http://www.opensiteexplorer.org/
- http://piwik.org/
- http://www.hittail.com/
- http://blumenthals.com/blog/2011/03/15/infographic-owning-your-local-web-equity/
- http://www.eloqua.com/
- http://www.marketo.com/
- http://www.trackur.com/
- http://www.link-assistant.com/

5.0 Online Marketing Program Summation

For ease of understanding what it is we're presenting here, can be understood by our following Infographic – our Pyramid to Online Marketing Success!

What can be seen from this program is that for a website to be a successful revenue generator for any online entrepreneur or firm, is that you must remember the following mantra – *"that the web is built on engagement leading to conversion."*

If you start with a great aesthetically looking, navigable website that offers up your products/services with the appropriate call to action – you will gain conversions based on the traffic that your SEO campaign brings. Add in the daily use of social media to become a respected online authority in your channel and the further reputation that comes with building your social community to reinforce and own your channel.

Which means of course, that if you use the basic foundation tasks that we've outlined herein, all timed as shown, that you can and you will build that revenue stream. It is truly not easy, nor for that matter is it a process that once laid out remains a constant as it changes with a regularity that is both impossible to gauge or to predict.

Staying current is perhaps one of the most persistent characteristics of an online marketer – it's the true measure of those who are successful, and this online marketing program can help any online entrepreneur be up at the leading edge.

So follow this online marketing strategy, educate yourself and you will find that honest hard work will pay off in the end...and follow our mantra....

Read...learn...hypothesize...test...analyze.... to Rank!

6.0 Credits...

Jim Rudnick -- MCSD

- **CEO ~ KKT INTERACTIVE**

- **a Microsoft Certified Solution Developer**

- **more than 18 years of SEO experience**

- **with more than 25 years of web experience**

- **have worked for NY Yankees, PEP Boys, GE, The Disney Company, Canada Life,**

    Mercedes, SAAB, Reuters and Quaker State Oil...

- **built more than 400 sites...& run more than 100 SEO Campaigns**

- **we build sites that have had millions of hits come up on the first page in**

    search engines and more than that – we build sites that generate new

    business for our clients day after day!!!

- **we blog about Canadian SEO at www.canuckseo.com**

Please contact the author, Jim Rudnick at
jrudnick@kkti.com or (905) 928-5566

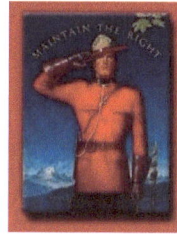

KKI INTERACTIVE   **CanuckSEO.com**

www.ingramcontent.com/pod-product-compliance
Lightning Source LLC
Chambersburg PA
CBHW041713200326
41519CB00001B/151